107

A Note to Parents and Caregivers:

Read-it! Joke Books are for children who are moving ahead on the amazing road to reading. These fun books support the acquisition and extension of reading skills as well as a love of books.

Published by the same company that produces *Read-it!* Readers, these books introduce the question/answer and dialogue patterns that help children expand their thinking about language structure and book formats.

When sharing joke books with a child, read in short stretches. Pause often to talk about the meaning of the jokes. The question/answer and dialogue formats work well for this purpose and provide an opportunity to talk about the language and meaning of the jokes. Have the child turn the pages and point to the pictures and familiar words. When you read the jokes, have fun creating the voices of characters or emphasizing some important words. Be sure to reread favorite jokes.

There is no right or wrong way to share books with children. Find time to read with your child, and pass on the legacy of literacy.

Adria F. Klein, Ph.D.
Professor Emeritus
California State University
San Bernardino, California

Editor: Christianne Jones
Designer: Joe Anderson
Creative Director: Keith Griffin
Editorial Director: Carol Jones
Managing Editor: Catherine Neitge
Page Production: Picture Window Books
The illustrations in this book were created digitally.

Picture Window Books
5115 Excelsior Boulevard
Suite 232
Minneapolis, MN 55416
877-845-8392
www.picturewindowbooks.com

Printed in the United States of America.

Library of Congress Cataloging-in-Publication Data
Ziegler, Mark, 1954-
Mind knots : a book of riddles / by Mark Ziegler ; illustrated by Ryan Haugen.
p. cm. — (Read-it! joke books—supercharged!)
ISBN 1-4048-1162-1 (hard cover)
1. Riddles, Juvenile. I. Haugen, Ryan, 1972- II. Title. III. Series.

PN6371.5.Z483 2006
818'.602–dc22   2005004069

Mind Knots

A Book of Riddles

by Mark Ziegler   illustrated by Ryan Haugen

Special thanks to our advisers for their expertise:

Adria F. Klein, Ph.D.
Professor Emeritus, California State University
San Bernardino, California

Susan Kesselring, M.A.
Literacy Educator
Rosemount–Apple Valley–Eagan (Minnesota) School District

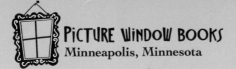

PICTURE WINDOW BOOKS
Minneapolis, Minnesota

What travels around the world, but stays in one corner?
A postage stamp.

Why did the scientist put a knocker at his front door?
To win the no bell prize.

Why is it always cold at the end of the year?
Because it's Decembrrrrrrrrr!

What is the world's laziest mountain?
Mount Everest.

What falls without making any noise?
Night.

What did the puppy say when it climbed on top of the house?
"Roof!"

What's the last thing you take off before you go to bed?
Your feet off the floor.

What gets wet the more it dries?
A towel.

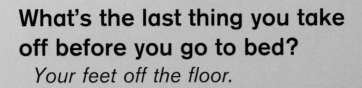

What can you hold without touching?
Your breath.

What kind of ship never sinks?
Friendship.

What do you call a pelican that doesn't fly?
A pelican't.

What kind of fur do you get from a skunk?
As fur away as possible!

How many chickens can you put in an empty box?

One. After that, the box isn't empty anymore!

What has four legs but cannot walk?
A table.

What do you call a sheep covered in chocolate?
A candy baaaaaa.

What do whales like to chew?
Blubber gum.

How do you catch a school of fish?
With a bookworm.

Why were the suspenders arrested?
For holding up the pants.

What is faster—heat or cold?
Heat. You can always catch cold.

How many feet are in a yard?
Depends on how many people are standing in it.

What can you put in a barrel to make it lighter?
Holes.

What letters are not in the alphabet?
The ones in the mail.

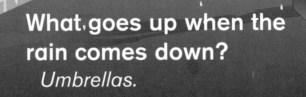

What goes up when the rain comes down?
Umbrellas.

Why don't bananas go sunbathing?
Because they always peel.

What kind of bow cannot be tied?
A rainbow.

What can you break with just a whisper?
Silence.

What does a piece of toast wear to bed?
Jammies.

**What grows down
when it grows up?**
  A duck.

**What has bark but
never bites?**
  A tree.

What starts with T, ends with T, and is filled with T?
A teapot.

How much is a skunk worth?
A "scent."

What keys cannot open doors?

Turkeys, monkeys, and donkeys.

What do elves learn in school?

The elfabet.

**What has lots of teeth
but cannot eat?**
A comb.

**What room has no windows
and no doors?**
A mushroom.

**What goes
ooh-la-la-
buzz-buzz?**
French flies.

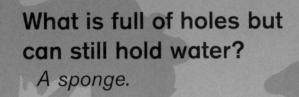

**What is full of holes but
can still hold water?**
A sponge.

**What pet makes the
loudest sound?**
A trumpet.

Where do polar bears go to dance?
A snowball.

Why did the clock get sick?
It was run down.

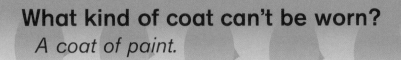

What kind of coat can't be worn?
A coat of paint.

What kind of ring is always square?
A boxing ring.

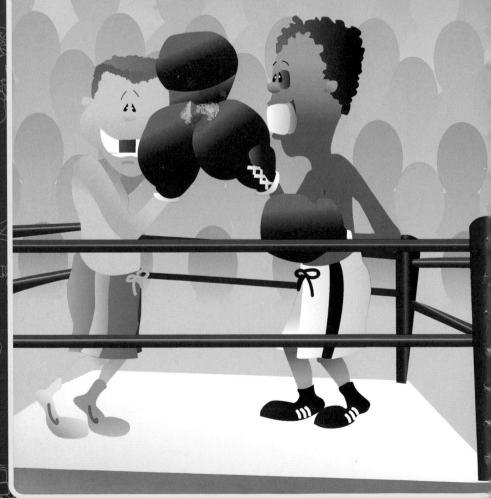

Why did the girl sit on the watch?
She wanted to be on time.

What can you serve but never eat?
A volleyball.

What does a baby computer call its father?
Data.

Read-it! Joke Books— Supercharged!

Beastly Laughs: A Book of Monster Jokes by Michael Dahl

Chalkboard Chuckles: A Book of Classroom Jokes by Mark Moore

Chitchat Chuckles: A Book of Funny Talk by Mark Ziegler

Creepy Crawlers: A Book of Bug Jokes by Mark Moore

Critter Jitters: A Book of Animal Jokes by Mark Ziegler

Fur, Feathers, and Fun! A Book of Animal Jokes by Mark Ziegler

Giggle Bubbles: A Book of Underwater Jokes by Mark Ziegler

Goofballs! A Book of Sports Jokes by Mark Ziegler

Lunchbox Laughs: A Book of Food Jokes by Mark Ziegler

Nutty Names: A Book of Name Jokes by Mark Ziegler

Roaring with Laughter: A Book of Animal Jokes by Michael Dahl

School Kidders: A Book of School Jokes by Mark Ziegler

Sit! Stay! Laugh! A Book of Pet Jokes by Michael Dahl

Spooky Sillies: A Book of Ghost Jokes by Mark Moore

Wacky Wheelies: A Book of Transportation Jokes by Mark Ziegler

Wacky Workers: A Book of Job Jokes by Mark Ziegler

What's up, Doc? A Book of Doctor Jokes by Mark Ziegler

Looking for a specific title or level? A complete list
of *Read-it!* Readers is available on our Web site:
www.picturewindowbooks.com